Simple Machines

What Is a Plane?

By Lloyd G. Douglas

Children's Press®
A Division of Scholastic Inc.
New York / Toronto / London / Auckland / Sydney
Mexico City / New Delhi / Hong Kong
Danbury, Connecticut

Photo Credits: Cover and all photos by Maura B. McConnell
Contributing Editor: Jennifer Silate
Book Design: Mindy Liu

Library of Congress Cataloging-in-Publication Data

Douglas, Lloyd G.
What is a plane? / by Lloyd G. Douglas.
   p. cm. — (Simple machines)
  Includes index.
  Summary: Describes simple machines called planes or ramps and how they
  are used to make work easier.
  ISBN 0-516-23964-3 (library binding) — ISBN 0-516-24023-4 (paperback)
  1. Ramps (Walkways)—Juvenile works. 2. Inclined planes—Juvenile
  literature. [1. Inclined planes.] I. Title.

TH2259 .D68 2002
621.8'11--dc21

2002001410

Contents

A **plane** is a **simple machine**.

It is a flat, **sloped surface**.

Planes help to make work easier.

The plane makes lifting the heavy boxes onto the truck easier.

This **ramp** is also a plane.

The ramp is easier to use than stairs.

People who use **wheelchairs** use a ramp instead of stairs.

11

Planes are used in many places.

This boat docks at a plane that goes over water.

People use the plane to get off the boat.

Planes are all around us.

Can you find the plane on the **playground**?

The **slide** is a plane.

When you go down a slide, you move fast.

Planes are very important simple machines.

They are used for many things.

21

New Words

plane (**plane**) a flat surface that helps us move things from place to place

playground (**play**-ground) an outdoor area, often with swings, slides, seesaws, and other things where children can play

ramp (**ramp**) a leaning surface that links a high place with a low place

simple machine (**sim**-puhl muh-**sheen**) a basic mechanical device that makes work easier

slide (**slide**) a smooth surface on which people can move

sloped (**slohpt**) at an angle

surface (**sur**-fiss) the outside of something

wheelchairs (**weel**-chairz) chairs on wheels for people who cannot walk

To Find Out More

Books
Inclined Planes and Wedges
by Sally M. Walker
Lerner Publications

Ramps and Wedges
by Angela Royston
Heinemann Library

Web Site
Simple Machines
http://www.coe.uh.edu/archive/science/science_lessons/
    scienceles1/finalhome.htm
Learn about and do experiments with simple machines on this
Web site.

Index

About the Author
Lloyd G. Douglas is an editor and writer of children's books.

Reading Consultants
Kris Flynn, Coordinator, Small School District Literacy, The San Diego County Office of Education

Shelly Forys, Certified Reading Recovery Specialist, W.J. Zahnow Elementary School, Waterloo, IL

Sue McAdams, Former President of the North Texas Reading Council of the IRA, and Early Literacy Consultant, Dallas, TX

WARREN TOWNSHIP LIBRARY
42 MOUNTAIN BLVD.
WARREN, NJ 07059